What's in this book

学习内容 Contents

读一读 Read

听听说说 Listen and say 12

写一写 Write 16

多元学习 Connections 18

温习 Checkpoint 20

分享 Sharing 22

This book belongs to

____

奥运会 The Olympic Games

学习内容 Contents

沟通 Communication

说说体育运动
Talk about sports

生词 New words

★	最	most
★	开始	to start
★	第	(marker of ordinal numerals
★	号	date
★	跑	to run
★	走	to walk
★	快	fast
	体育	sport
	篮球	basketball
	羽毛球	badminton
	跳	to jump
	慢	slow

句式 Sentence patterns

希腊举办了最早的奥林匹克运动会。
The very first Olympic Games were held in Greece.

跨学科学习 Project

搜集一位奥运会奖牌得主的资料并介绍他/她
Research an Olympic medal winner and talk about him/her

文化 Cultures

北京奥运会
Beijing Olympic Games

Get ready

1 Do you know what these buildings are?

2 Do you know what events were held in these buildings?

3 Do you like watching sports events?

读一读 Read

776 BC

zuì zǎo de
最早的

两三千年前，希腊举办了最早的奥林匹克运动会（奥运会）。

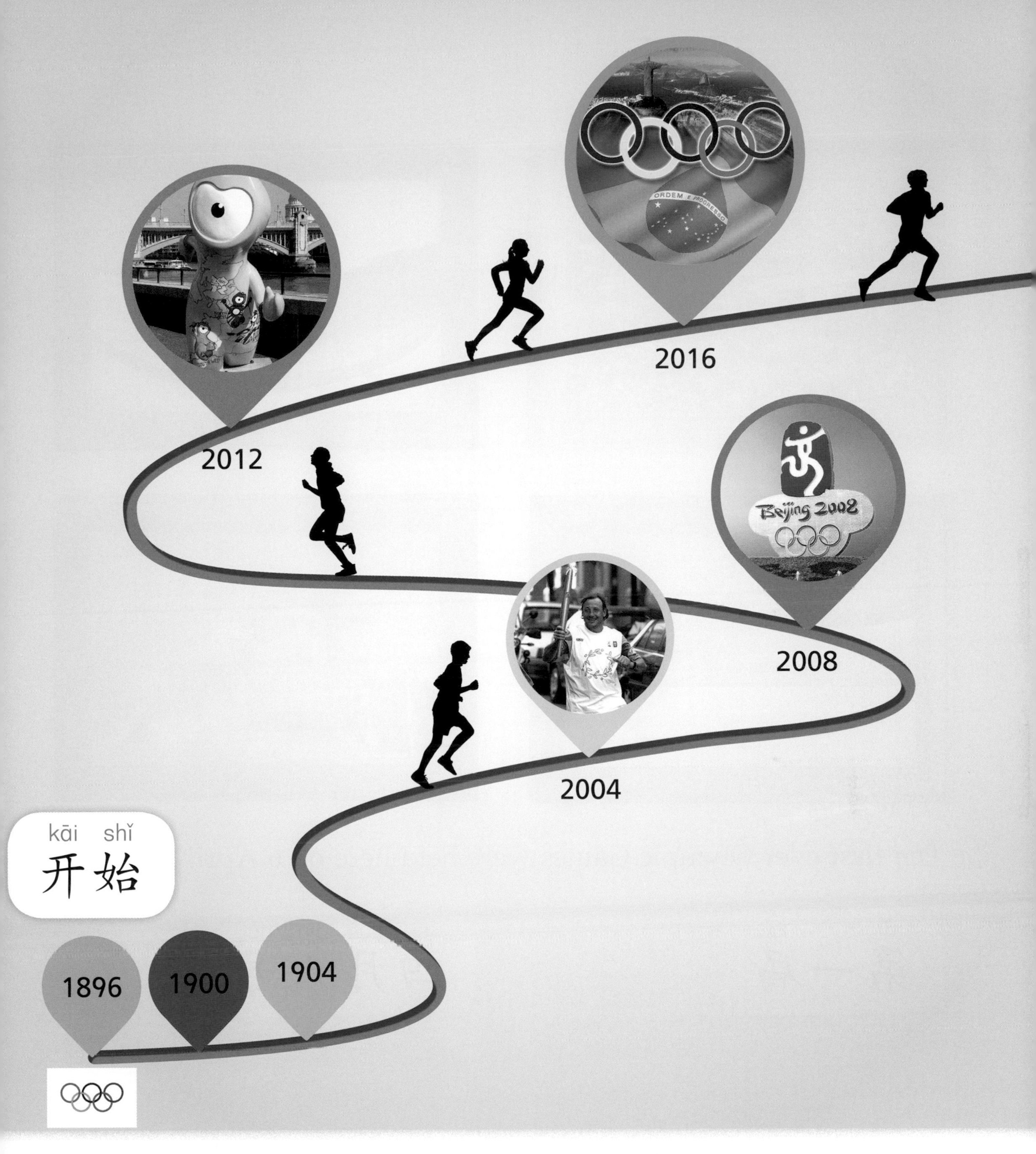

现代奥运会在一百多年前开始举办，每四年一届。

The **first** ever Olympic Games were held here on **6 April** 1896.

dì yī jiè
第一届

sì yuè liù hào
四月六号

第一届在一八九六年四月六号举行，也是在希腊。

今天，奥运会的体育项目有四十多个。

篮球、羽毛球、跳高、跑步、竞走……你都可以在奥运会上看到。

不管是男还是女，是快还是慢，大家都是好朋友。

Let's think

1 Which one of these is the symbol of the Olympic Games? Circle the correct letter.

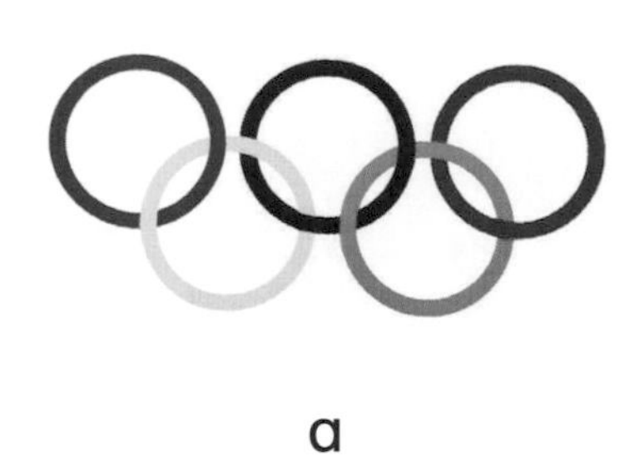

a

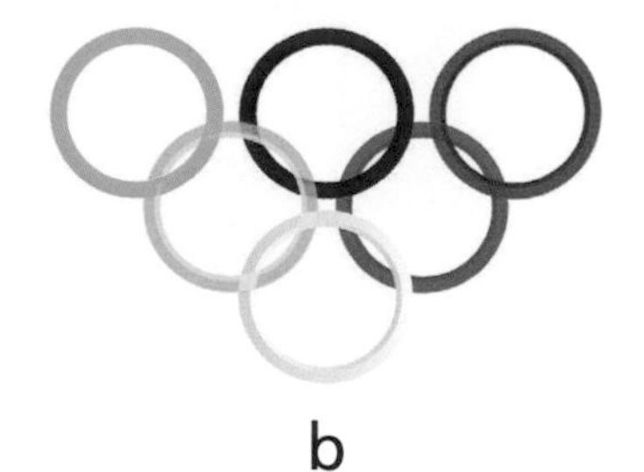

b

c

2 Write the years of the Olympic Games.

2004 2008 2012

3 What are the children doing? Tick the Olympic sports.

New words

1 Learn the new words.

2 Listen to your teacher and act out the words.

听听说说 Listen and say

1 Listen and tick the correct pictures.

1

2

3

2 Look at the pictures. Listen to the story an

一、二、三，开始！

谁最快？

长颈鹿，你个子高，你打篮球。
猴子，你喜欢跳，你打羽毛球。

你看，马最快，跑第一。老虎跑第二。

老虎怎么比马慢？

狮子爷爷，您慢慢走。

我最慢，你们都比我快。

3 Write the letters. Role-play with your friend.

a 走　b 跑　c 跳　d 篮球

1

2

3

4

Task

What sports do you and your friends like? Do a survey and write your names.

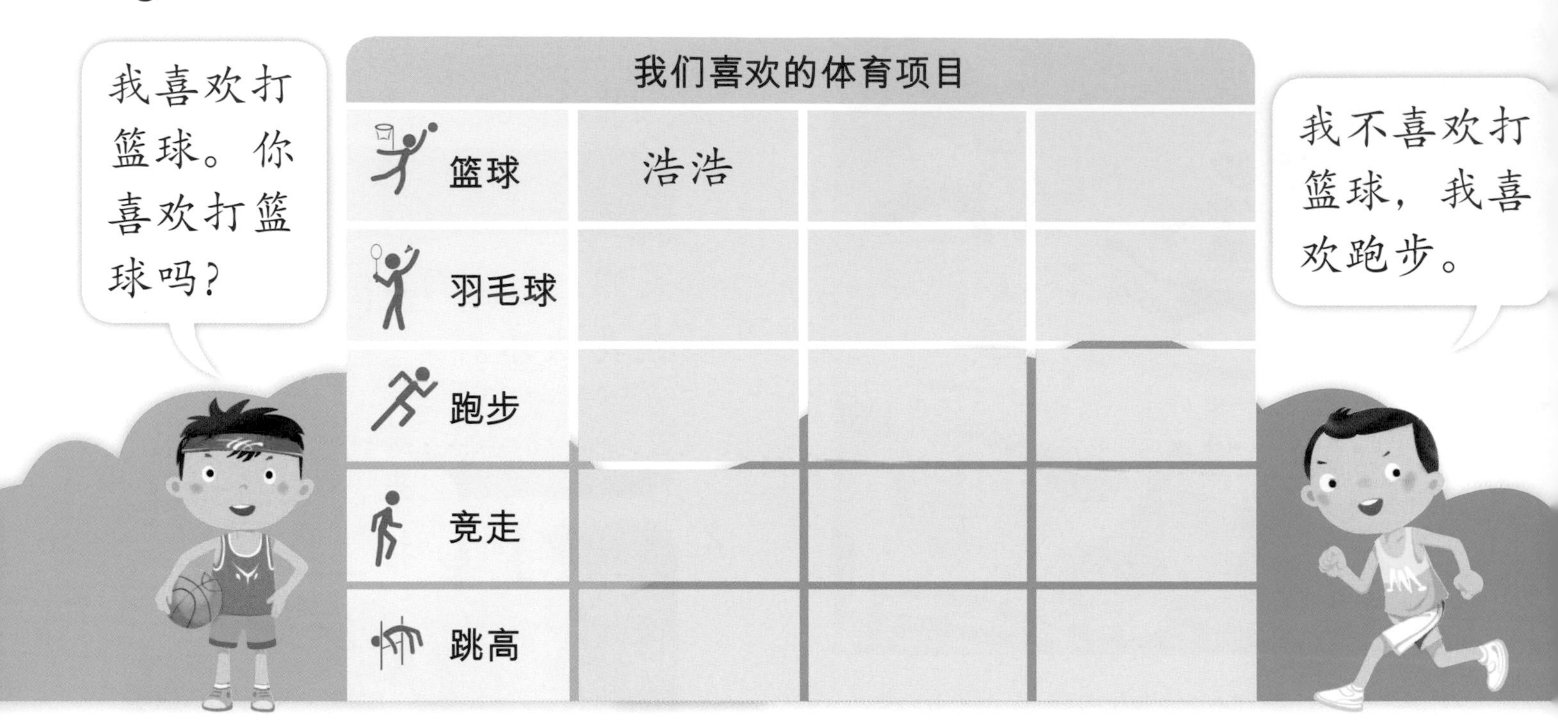

我们喜欢的体育项目			
篮球	浩浩		
羽毛球			
跑步			
竞走			
跳高			

Game

Listen to your teacher. Repeat the words in white. For the ones in black, repeat and act them out.

Chant

Listen and say.

多做运动身体好，

真呀真开心！

我们一起来赛跑，

看谁第一名。

你跑得快，我跑得慢，

第一第二第三名。

大家一起来赛跑，

真呀真开心！

生活用语 Daily expressions

写一写 Write

1 Trace and write the characters.

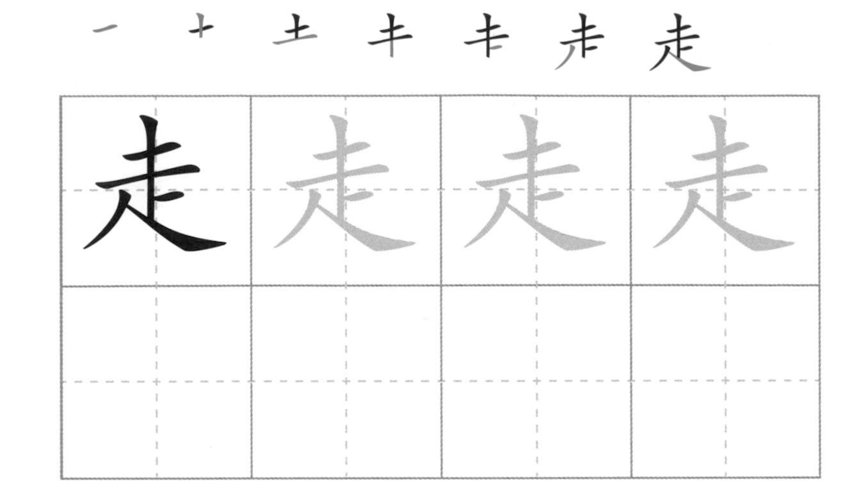

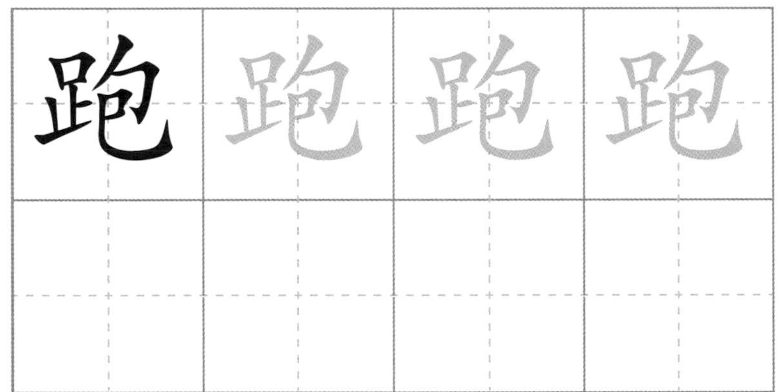

2 Write and say.

他一 ___。
他喜欢 ___。

她三 ___。
她喜欢 ___。

3 Read and circle the wrong words, then write the correct ones. There is one mistake in each line.

星期六晚上，伊森、艾文和 1 ______
浩浩一起在公园玩。艾文走在最 2 ______
前面。浩浩第一，在艾文后面。 3 ______
伊森走在最后面，他是第三。 4 ______
艾文很高兴，因为她最快。 5 ______

拼音输入法 Pinyin input

Circle the wrong characters in the messages and choose the correct ones. Write the letters.

a 画画 b 笔 c 马

In Pinyin input, tones are usually not required. Therefore, one Pinyin syllable can generate a list of characters with different tones. Because of this, it is important to remember the form of the desired character.

1

2

3

Cultures

1 The 2008 Olympic Games were held in Beijing. Learn about the Games.

Beijing 2008

From 8 to 24 August, 10,942 athletes from 204 countries and areas competed in 302 events.

The main venues

the Beijing National Stadium (the Bird's Nest)

the Beijing National Aquatics Centre (the Water Cube)

2 Do you know the five mascots? Their names form the sentence 'bei jing huan ying ni', which means 'welcome to Beijing'. Match them to the animals/element they represent.

Beibei

Jingjing

Huanhuan

Yingying

Nini

Project

1 When did these athletes win their gold medals in the Olympic Games? Do an online research. Then match them to their names. Write the letters.

a Lin Dan b Roger Federer c Usain Bolt d Yelena Isinbayeva

2 Research an Olympic medal winner that you like. Paste his/her photo and tell your friend about him/her.

Paste the photo here.

我最喜欢……
他/她很高/矮/胖/瘦。
他/她的脸圆圆的/方方的。
他/她会跑步/打球/跳高/……
……年，他/她是第一/二/三。

温习 Checkpoint

1 Say the words and the sentences and write the characters. Then draw your face on one of the pictures on the right.

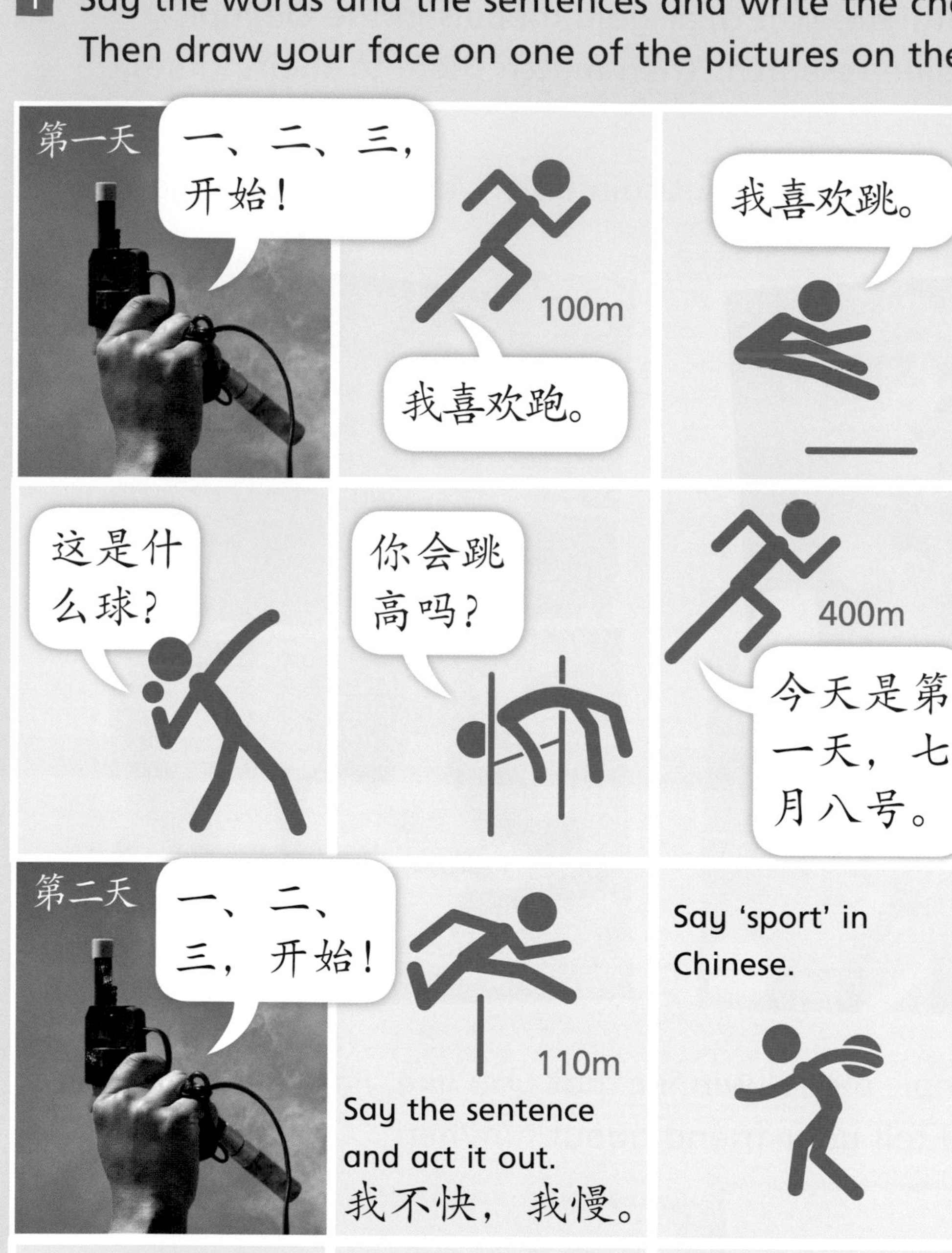

Say 'the ninth' in Chinese.

Write the character.

Write the character.

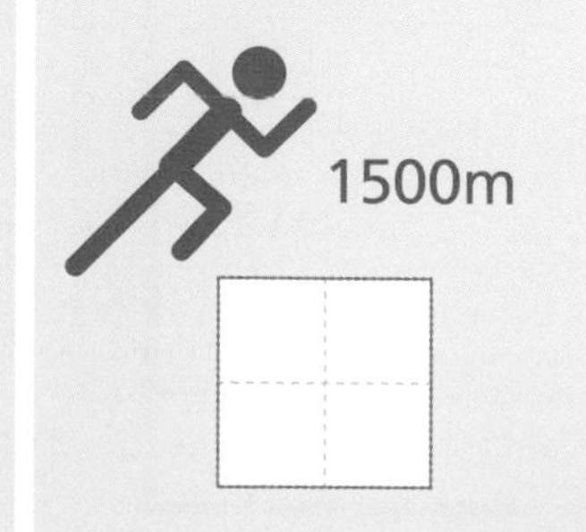

我跑步第一！我真快乐。

这是我的。我跳高第一！

2 Work with your friend. Colour the stars and the chillies.

Words	说	读	写
最	☆	☆	🌶
开始	☆	☆	🌶
第	☆	☆	🌶
号	☆	☆	🌶
跑	☆	☆	☆
走	☆	☆	☆
快	☆	☆	☆
体育	☆	🌶	🌶
篮球	☆	🌶	🌶

Words and sentences	说	读	写
羽毛球	☆	🌶	🌶
跳	☆	🌶	🌶
慢	☆	🌶	🌶
希腊举办了最早的奥林匹克运动会。	☆	🌶	🌶

Talk about sports	☆

3 What does your teacher say?

分享 Sharing

Words I remember

最	zuì	most
开始	kāi shǐ	to start
第	dì	(marker of ordinal numbers
号	hào	date
跑	pǎo	to run
走	zǒu	to walk
快	kuài	fast
体育	tǐ yù	sport
篮球	lán qiú	basketball
羽毛球	yǔ máo qiú	badminton
跳	tiào	to jump
慢	màn	slow

Other words

前	qián	before
希腊	xī là	Greece
举办	jǔ bàn	to host, to hold
奥林匹克运动会	ào lín pǐ kè yùn dòng huì	the Olympic Games
现代	xiàn dài	modern
多	duō	more than
每	měi	every
届	jiè	session
举行	jǔ xíng	to hold
项目	xiàng mù	event
跳高	tiào gāo	high jump
跑步	pǎo bù	running
竞走	jìng zǒu	race walk
可以	kě yǐ	to be able to
不管	bù guǎn	regardless of

Oxford University Press is a department of the University of Oxford.
It furthers the University's objective of excellence in research, scholarship,
and education by publishing worldwide. Oxford is a registered trade mark of
Oxford University Press in the UK and in certain other countries

Published in Hong Kong by
Oxford University Press (China) Limited
39th Floor, One Kowloon, 1 Wang Yuen Street, Kowloon Bay,
Hong Kong

First Edition published in 2017

Illustrated by Anne Lee, Ah Lun, KY Chan and Wildman

Photographs for reproduction permitted by Dreamstime.com

China National Publications Import & Export (Group) Corporation is an authorized distributor of
Oxford Elementary Chinese.

Please contact content@cnpiec.com.cn or 86-10-65856782

ISBN: 978-0-19-942996-7

10 9 8 7 6 5 4 3 2